FROM
PINK
BOWS
TO
RED
STILETTOS

FROM PINK BOWS TO RED STILETTOS

Xia Devore

iUniverse, Inc.
Bloomington

From Pink Bows to Red Stilettos

iUniverse books may be ordered through booksellers or by contacting:

iUniverse
1663 Liberty Drive
Bloomington, IN 47403
www.iuniverse.com
1-800-Authors (1-800-288-4677)

ISBN: 978-1-4759-8179-7 (sc)
ISBN: 978-1-4759-8180-3 (ebk)

Printed in the United States of America

iUniverse rev. date: 03/15/2013

Coming Soon by
Xia Devore
Cami and Friends: Erotic Tales

Xia Devore would like to hear your taste on her seductive outlook on life. Feel free to email Xia at xia@xiadevore.com. You may also visit her website at www.xiadevore.com.

Table of Contents

Dedication

This is dedicated to the "Xia Devore Support Team,"

and in remembrance of the one person, who felt I could always be whatever I so desired.

"Love is sometimes earned and then . . . there's unconditional love."

Acknowledgments

This process has been a long and arduous task yet a dreamy and gratifying process. I would like to first thank my Eagle, who offered life back to my poetic mind and voice after years of my pen lying tranquil and stagnant.

I would like to thank the entire "Xia Devore Support Team." A magnificent group of family and friends who would not allow my ink well to dry and offered much inspiration for the continuous flow of my erotic thoughts to spill onto these pages. Especially thanking each of you, for offering positive and negative criticism and more than 5 hours of energy to me.

I would also like to give much gratitude to my Business Savvy Team, who knew the ends and outs of such a production. Your support in discouraging any doubts and expanding my knowledge, made this journey well worth it.

A round of applause for my Redding XD Connect, a literary genius I call friend, who took time from her busy schedule and family to edit this work. Your time and opinions are seen and greatly appreciated throughout this work. You have always been and continue to be of great value to me.

To my second editor, the "Ultimate Kat Daddy," it was a joy to reconnect and brainstorm together. I say to you, we sometimes find ourselves in bizarre situations but remember, "Timing is Everything."

Much love to Xia Devore Junior, who understood mommy's time away from her motherly duties to bring this book to life, despite her understanding of this so called "Adult Literature." Mommy loves you!!!

Thanks to iUniverse Publishing Company for evolving From Pink Bows to Red Stilettos. Thanks to my first point of contact, Courtney Mathews, who was threatened with a red stiletto if she would steal my work and was filled with laughter from my brutal humor. To my consultants, who answered every necessary and burdensome question I posed, your help was greatly appreciated!

Last but not least, thanks to Start Graphics for helping design and brand the Xia Devore experience for readers and viewers delight.

Preface

From Pink Bows to Red Stilettos is a rich portrayal of the seductive tongue of a little girl who once danced around with pink bows in her hair and now slips on her red stilettos, tantalizing the desires of the men she meets. Through written word that leaves one craving for something more, From Pink Bows to Red Stilettos unleashes raw, sexual, provocative, taboo style poetry to appease your sexual senses and fundamental sexual literary cravings. From Pink Bows to Red Stilettos proves that a woman's sexual provocative nature is nothing to take lightly and that a sweet little girl can grow up to have a burning tigress nature. Whether enjoyed in private or shared with friends, lovers, or partners, this girl's tongue will paint a vivid picture of the nights she's lived and the simultaneous joys she has experienced from his mouth to hers.

Deep Roots, Spicy Life

Where I'm from?
Is not exactly the trees
It's more like the stalks
Sugar cane to be precise
Me and my peeps . . .
Are sweet and nice
Kissing the Gulf of Mexico
Tonguing hurricane threats
We back dat ass up
'Til our men drip sweat
Stripping off our clothes
Speaking in a Cajun dialect
Gumbo and Creole cuisine
Lewd and breast baring acts
Bourbon Street and swinging legs
Naked women and hand grenades
Street performers and walkers alike
We don't care about your sexuality
You can do what you like
In the street or behind closed doors
Every freaking day
And every freaking night
The choice is yours
Either way is considered polite
Cayenne pepper is who I am
The true reason why I write
South Louisiana, baby
Cajun Blood, Cajun Spice!

Writer's Unblocked

He asked to be in my book of poetry
Could I write some lyrics just for him?
Stumped with writer's block
I grant him the opportunity he suggest
He paints my toes with his sweet saliva
With his tongue he wets my scalp
He covers everything in between the two
Then ask . . . "Was that enough to inspire you?
Cause I adore you . . . through and through"
In awe from this inspiration
Ink wets my paper
As ferociously as he devoured me
In spite of my reservation
He was just the motivation I needed
For this poetry to take flight
And my writer's block to go unheeded

From Pink Bows to Red Stilettos

He's visualizing a sight
I can't seem to view
His jaw drops in awe
As his thoughts begin to stew
I once was a youthful girl
Out of his reach and undesired too
Yet now a woman
Hardly to be called a youth
See . . . he's 15 years my senior
Once a school girl's crush
Forbidden thoughts of him
Spawned a young girl to lust
Seeing him after all these years
Well . . . it's just perfect for us
I'm now sporting Red Stilettos
He can't wait to touch
With eyes of disbelief
He marvels at my transformed figure
Voluptuous is the part once called chest
That frame obviously now holds breast
I've lost the title "Stick"
As he notices, I'm swaying a pair of hips
Walking with a strut
Ass going . . . Pow!!!
Yes . . . I'm all grown up
Catching the eyes of older men . . .
And any young pup
Legs extended to the sky
My conversation considered fly
I'm now a ravishing beauty
A sculpture to behold
He's lost the vision of my Pink Bows
Sternly requesting me in Red Stilettos

Live Instrumentation

He's my conductor
And I . . . his orchestra
Finessing my keys
Walking his fingers thru my strings
Licking only two
Then strumming my clit
I am his every instrument
A sound of beauty emits
Up and down with his stick
He beats my drum
Bottoms out my bass
Melody in sync
Engaging my valves
Lowering my pitch
We trumpet to triumph
Notes penned to paper
The title of this work
The sounds of love making
Or just the harmony of lust
Live instrumentation
A song between us

The Gold Pack

Ladies, my ladies
Can we talk about the gold pack?
Can we talk about the gold pack?
You know the one with black writing
A true indicator of something large
Gripping the sausage in its casing
Reaping havoc in your insides
A radiant beauty to behold
Colossal, magnificent . . . certified gold

Ladies, my ladies
Can we talk about the gold pack?
But now this time . . . with the slack
Often misused and abused
Fellows, it's not your size
You are dazed and confused
If in the act it slips . . .
And I have to wear it in me
It's not your size
You should not be surprised
Excessive space at the tip
Should've been your guide

Fellows, my fellows
I'm now talking to you guys
The gold pack, the gold pack
Stop filling your head with lies
If your prophylactic is lax
It is not your rubber size
We ladies don't ask for much
But listen to me guys
Please do us ladies a favor
And by your damn size!

I Make It Look Easy

I found myself in a city I had never been
Who am I kidding?
It's where Xia Devore really begins
And this time, I had something on my mind
A dubious plan as I hit the streets
Stopping the first duck I meet
His shirt says, "I Make It Look Easy"
I'm ready to put him to the test
His downtown loft only a block away
I'm green and naive, following his lead
To the 8th floor we soar
Educated conversation, as scholars we learn more
Yet, one is thinking "I'm smarter"
With each minute growing hotter
The outline of his tool appears to be getting harder
A waterfall is beginning, eagerly awaiting his drilling
Safety first, Jimmy hat required
Before he breaks on through to the other side
And oh yes, he have talent
Although, his entire tool is too much to handle
The head alone causes the escape of my bellows
He covers my mouth and says, "I have neighbors"
I bite his fingers and sing, "Do me baby"
Climax builds and the energy of the room felt strange
He was in so much control until our location changed
An epiphany he has as he processed this plight
What woman does this shit . . . after midnight?
His eyebrow arose realizing the hidden agenda
He'd been picked, plucked, and fucked by the opposite gender

Job Hunting

He's lost his job
Sitting with face in hands
I shudder at his pain
So, I kneel before my king
My fingers unzip his pants
Taking his knob between my lips
Stroking with my mouth
His head begins to drift
To the back of the chair
Eyes closed, he begins to smirk
I suck harder and he smiles
He loves when I go to work
Music always lifts his spirits
So, I begin to hum
As my mouth bobbles his left nut
Then the right, he's having fun
I have to see this task all the way through
He deserves to cum
I return to deep throating
And his eyes open for this one
He secretes his pains into my mouth
With jaws full of sorrow
I swallow this day's agony
Job hunting begins tomorrow

Traditional

Roses are red
Violets are blue
He says I'm too much for one
But not enough for two
Yet, little does he know
If he keeps bringing his boy around
I'll be fucking him too

Masterpiece

Deliberately waiting for him to get home
He's looking forward to exercising
I'm thinking of other calisthenics
He opens the door
There I stand in the foyer
In only a black and white fit
Pearls and stilettos
Showing a facial expression of puzzlement
He questions my garb
Feeling his back was against the wall
He utters . . . "You want paint . . . I'll paint"
He scoops me up and carries me off
Dropping me on his bed canvas
Priming me with his mouth
Then, brushing with strokes of bold colors
Turning my flesh red until we both release white
We lay back in awe of this masterpiece
Unexpected . . . but right

IHOD

Once possessed by the American Boy
This pussy never doubted his ability
Until growing tired of what he employed
Seeking real love . . . I was deployed
Never leaving my country
But finding global love within
Latin Lovers and French Ticklers
Italian Stallions and Aussies Down Under
Dark men who respect my beauty
And the genuineness of my blend
Once called, "The American Chick"
More suitably christened
"International House of Dicks"

Platter

Now, I've never been one for the munchies
But he reminds me of a Chef
He appears to be cooking up something
A masterpiece at its best
We find ourselves in the kitchen
Oven preheating for our meal
I'm intrigued by his apron
Reading "This Cooks the Real Deal"
Questioning his culinary skills
The sink now my prop
Displaying technique in his craft
This cooks already reached my G spot
Marinating with his juices
To the table with his spread
With tongue drooling
His face ravaging my plate
This Southern Chef, ate . . . and he ate
With his main course now complete
I'm left craving something sweet

Clearing My Desk

One grueling day at work
This day will never end
Everyone has gone home
I'm the only one left in
My head lifts from my desk
A vision of love appears
He informs me that my work is over
And he will take it from here
Moving me behind my desk
Lifting my rump from my chair
He gently lays out his project before him
Applying a hot compress of passionate kisses
His finger slips under my skirt
Meddling in my love nest
It's wet to his liking
His dick is inserted next
He calls it his "day is over" stick
Flawlessly it flexes
Papers are flying everywhere
The phone is off the hook
Computer buttons being pressed
We can't catch our breath
Caught up in this intense moment
An orgasm is all we have left
Our sap wets the desk
My calendar is now ruined
But this day I won't forget
Burning the midnight oil
May well be worth it!

One Finger, Two

Jaded and home alone
But all the while I have a plan
Soft music, fragrant candles
The operation of my hand
One finger, then another
Memorizing my vacant land
Slow grinding of my cat
To my own rhythmic jam
Wrist popping, pat . . . pat . . . pat
'Til my wetness breaks the dam

Gusto

Today is the day I go for the gusto
He packs an ocean variety of goods
With me showing no fear for his terms of endearment
A dress is my attire for this event
No undergarments will make an entrance
Smiling upon arrival, kissing the back of my neck as usual
No need to say it, I automatically toot that ass up for his frisking
He lifts my dress and discovers a pantyless feline
As I await his vessel from my stern
He's the Captain of this cruise ship
He navigates just below sea level
Yet his boat always rises to perfection
Touring my canal with true conviction
As he pins and pegs my bow to the settee
My legs begin to rock from the impact
He pops me in the small of my torso
And says, "Get that arch back"
He's stroking with emotion, rolling in my ocean
The strides that he takes, causes my waves to break
Tides are rising as my love begins to crash down
I'm engulfed with enthusiasm, feeling I'm about to drown
Submarined to the floor, as I can go no more
Five minutes lapse and we've drifted to a new position
Enlightened with a new vision, that begins with my keel
And needless to say, we're sailing with burning zeal

Nothing Last Long

Strangers meeting on an evening stroll
Intrigued by my hair, as I am his
With only one night to spare
In useless conversation we do not dwell
My hotel room seems the closest
Extended 27 floors above ground
Rendering a corner view
Spawning role play for us two
A perfect setting for matrimonial proposal
He drops to one knee
Popping the question with no ring
I'm astonished, accepting with glee
Saying yes to this man
I'm spending the rest of my life with . . .
Even if it's just for the night
A worthy engagement
He gets his fiancé right
Refusing to let me down
Diminishing to my lower extremity
Tongue lashing all around
Spinning into a 69
Legs shaking and twitching
The mood is just right
A sizable penis fills my empty site
Slowly pushing 'til I seize his dick
No taping out, we refuse to quit
Husband material measures . . . tremendous
Curtains part revealing a break of sunlight
Rendering a feeling . . . simply horrendous
Forced to face the reality of last night's lies
Our engagement has ended
And we return to our daily lives

Weathering the Storm

It's raining cats and dogs
I'm ready for the storm
An umbrella kept for all types of weather
Guaranteed to protect from harm
Lifestyles and Durex
Trojans and Magnums
Just to name a few
When you get a weather alert
What's gonna protect you?

Smashville

After too long a wait, my Trojan appears
Having once whispered in my ear
"I wear a Magnum XL"
I understand this language
We officially speak the same dialect
I crave to feel this stallion
So, bring on the action!
In this classic country town
He makes one request I'm sure to deliver
Blue lace boy shorts and cowgirl boots
Greet him at the door
I'm all in for the big score
He begins his descend to my lower end
His tongue is immaculate
No preference of location
There's no fiction to this story
As I envelope him in my walls
I'm impressed with his coil
A Clydesdale to say the least
My fluids I release
Housekeeping desperately needed
Just to change the sheets
The noise I exclaim must cease
My dream is complete, his XL was real
As my lower extremity thumps and swells
In his pleasures I did not slight
We explored a lot of first throughout the night
Feeling the need to change up shit
Nashville is now Smashville, I firmly insist!

One Night

Not soon after I walked off from him
I see my new victim
And in seeing that ass
He knows he wants in
60 minutes of strong persuasion
Selling point being that it's thick and nice
Sold! My entrance is allowed
The screams are loud
The moans and groans proceeding
A shimmy in my leg and reverberation
The sensation from this lust
An explosion . . . yeah, I bet I bust
This bond between us
We should never disengage
My body convulses in a rage
As his stream overflows in my ocean
We spoon into a short slumber
Awakened by the sun, morning has come
Lazily, I arise and gaze in his eyes
To my surprise . . . he's still by my side

Timing is Everything

He's planned a special night for me
One that's sure to be filled with surprises
That starts when we arrive at the same time
Hand extended to knock on the door
We step back and give a once over
Her dress is the same black one as mine
As are the red shoes and the flowers in our hair
Startled by the note in our hands
We now possess the same puzzled look
The door is ajar and a voice says enter
We've both heard it before
The man that apparently makes us both quiver
He silences the argument, demanding our attention
He ask for peace tonight
A conversation with his two women
A meal fit for a queen he's prepared
Candles and mellow music fills the air
Dessert he feeds to both of us . . .
One plate enough to fill us both
He then escorts us to his room
A warm bath with flowers is now in view
We both give a look and before our mouths can speak
"Silence!!!" He says . . . "Tonight you're both with me"
Now, I've considered this experience, I cannot lie
But, had no idea this would be the night
I love this man . . . so, I follow his plight
Undressing us both . . . interchangeably
He then commands we disrobe him
As I wonder how this could be

We enter the tub and lift glasses of wine
As he toasts our grand union . . . between our three thighs
He starts kissing me then turns to her
I kiss his neck and he returns to me
This is starting out as one well conducted orchestra
She puts her hand on his penis then he slips his fingers in me
She goes to kiss him and he quickly moves
She's now kissing me
He rubs my breast and fingers her
She's kissing down my chest, as he suddenly grabs her
Shoving her face on his thick, hard cock
Commanding that I rise and place my cunt in his
This operation is so fast paced
I'm lost in my ideas
He moves my waist and lifts her from his
Saying, "Enjoy each other's love, we have so much to give"
I begin to suck her breast as she fingers me
Now we're passionately kissing
We seem to have lost he
He beckons us out of the bath and invites us to his bed
He says, "you don't need me, you girls use your heads"
We turn into a 69, licking around and round
He's seen enough . . . pointing . . . "YOU . . . it's time to ride!"
I slide on his dick and she on his face
We're fucking him to death
Orgasms all over the place
Excreting my final nut, I roll over in my space
Shaking and trembling, he fucks her into the same state
As she rolls to her side
Our king lies between us
He couldn't have planned a better night
We sleep until morning greets us

Silence Please

Bad day at work
I'm gunning for his ass
As soon as he opens the door
I begin to fuss and yap
He drops his lunch bucket
Givin' me the eye like . . .
He don't wanna hear that
Grabs me from the back
Demanding that I shut my trap
Rips my panties from under my skirt
Bends me over the kitchen table
Going straight to work
Giving me 3 strong minutes
Of the hardest sensual pumps
He skeets then I collapse
To only be followed by a pussy nap
As he stands over me, snarling
"The measures I have to go to . . .
Just to shut your trap"

Contents of Delight

Perched in his lap
As if it is Christmas
Mistletoe above
We begin kissing
No red suit or a jelly belly
Armor made of steel
A six pack of metal
Slowly swaying my back
I ride this daring machine
Tightly my legs strap
Titties he firmly squeeze
My drive becomes rapid
Then slowed by his touch
Fiddling with my clit
I pause to spurt a nut
Gathering my bearings
Returning to my stroke
Face pressed to his
Bodies almost one
Hands wrap my waist
Accelerating speed bumps
His smile turns to grimace
Love faces between us
My contents coming down
His skeet is shooting up
My pouch filled with joy
Squirted from his nuts

Trilogy

As the dew settles and the sun ascends
The sound of the padlock enters my ears
There is little opposition to this outlandish act
As a trifle through the bushes astonishes the cat
I am liberated by the oscillation felt in my earth
As my yard is trampled it vibrates the dirt
The synthesis of stupendous seduction calms my flame
Good morning to you, I hope tonight is the same

I attempt to be a novice as I begin my act
Lunch is only an hour so the thought I immediately retract
The method I have chosen to appease my hunger
Is etched with immaculate design built like no other
The apparatus is perfect as it causes my laboratory to explode
I applaud the climax as the apex is bestowed
Bewildered by this pleasure I'd press for more
But the clock continues to tick as it is time to find the door

Waxed and enthusiastic about the evening plans
Although vexed by difficulties I wanted this man
The feisty feline in me addresses the unknown of the night
Mauled by this carnivorous beast with pure delight
A nibble, a bite, my vulva devoured
My mouth roars a hideous howl
Like a beverage of ether, I am put into a state
To ebb into slumber, in the morning I awake

Hydraulics

My drink's nearing final sip
He's persistently talking shit
If he's trying to get this pussy tonight
He needs to shut the fuck up and hit it right
I'm in a 325 and he's pushing a Tahoe
No brainer . . . off to his truck we go
He says he's a driver
Well daddy . . . mami's a rider
So, I slide on his shift
Putting his hydraulics to test
Truck rocking and windows fogging
I'm bouncing as I do best
Punching overdrive on his dick
Head hitting the ceiling
'Til my neck feels a crick
This was a fantastic dealing
Now . . . are there any wet wipes in this bitch?!

Tick Tock Goes the Clock

Eyeballing the clock
For a perfect night planned
Yet, absent of my special man
Sitting in this chair
Staring at the door
Time tick tocks pass
The moment is no more
Music and wine kicking in
Eyes closed shut
Palms rubbing on my skin
Breast tender to the touch
With nipples like shooters
Only my stroke can expel
My hands just won't stop
Sliding below my waist
Left one massaging right breast
While the other enters my wet place
And I gently masturbate
Straddling my hand as I ride it
Pausing for just a moment
To caress and twiddle my clit
Juices trickle just a bit
My tune has taken over the room
When suddenly, I hear a sound
As he rushes in and meets my wet vulva
Surprised that his job is done
Disappointment spreads all over his face
Then, I stand to place . . .
My hands across his lips
In a whisper I say . . .
Time waits for no one
Clock hands never stay in place
If you have reservations
Next time . . . accommodate without haste

Faint Whispers

It appears I'm home alone
Hearing a faint whisper of my name
I emphatically search each room
Until only my bedroom remains
The sound from under my covers
Is slightly smothered and muffled
I flip back the sheets and it appears
Naked, cuffed, and waiting for early release
But he's to receive no credit for time served
There's always punishment for bad behavior
Slowly, I remove my belt,
And commence to spanking that fine ass
Intermittently undressing myself
Feeling sorry for the now wounded beast
I lick his wounds
And use my natural aloe to heal his hardness
Riding it frontwards, to the side, and then back
He squeaks and squeals a sound I've come to love
I release my ointment simultaneously with him
Overwhelming pleased, I sign his pardon
Spooning with him to a recuperation period
The house is overcome with silence

Expletives

He lays it so good
He invokes me to yell expletives
Fuck!!! Damn!!! This shit is so good!!!
He pumps that wood
As no other could
I scream his name
Oh yes . . . I bet the neighbors know his name
I have no shame
He yanked his saw from his pants
Cut me to shreds
One limb at time
Right foot, left foot
Left leg, right leg
Put the pussy to bed
Feeling that I'm dead
He rejuvenates me with a glass of water
And I oughta quit but shit
He's fiddling with my clit
Followed up by that lick
Expletives . . .
Fuck!!! Damn!!! Shit!!! That's my spot!!!
Feeling we are about to pull an all nighter
The pillows my new best friend
I bury my face within
This should be a sin
I hope this isn't hell
Cause if so . . . I'm all in

Rip and Tear

There's a dick I call "Rip and Tear"
You know the kind . . . that beat the clit 'til it hurts
Covers a pussy with lacerations
Painful urinations
When the drizzle roles down
Cause the dick was so big
You can hardly sit now
Deep flesh wounds
A medic is needed
Stitches may proceed it
But when asked if you would you do it again?
Your body hits rewind
Replaying it in your mind
An upward grin cannot deny
If the opportunity presents itself
"Rip and Tear" you will welcome any time

Hostage

She's looking at me as if he's my hostage
He's not being held against his will
Truth of the matter is
There's no ransom to give
It's elementary . . . my dear
The twat that I'm popping
Has increased his knowledge
You had him pushing up daisies
Nails in his coffin
Frankenstein . . . It's Alive!!!
Thriving betwixt my thighs
He's never coming home
Why do you look surprised?
He's found what he needed
Residing in my sexual paradise
Now all I have for you
Are tips and words of advice
Find you someone else
Better yet . . . sign up for my lessons
They're sure to pay off
Truly . . . a definite blessing

Against the Grain

The night is set, my water is ran
I couldn't ask for a better man
With a steadier hand
He's youthful and I'm his cougar
His skill is beyond his number
Always setting the stage for a new experience
He gently shaves my vagina
Only asking one question
"Can I cut against the grain?"
His words drive me insane
He inflicts no pain
His job is flawless
Washing it clean
Drying it gently
Only one task left
Thankful that it's his
Cause he eats the best

Freestyle

Big dicks are overrated
Nasty lickers are appreciated
Blowing in my ass is authenticated
Pussy so wet, it needs to be ventilated
He's already bust, so I'll just masturbate it

Sounds of Passion

Jazz playing between her thighs
Rustling of the sheets
Emitting a sound so exquisite
The neighbors sneak a peak
Bed clapping against the walls
As his thunder beats
Strumming all her strings
Fine tuning his masterpiece
Their harmony may be their doom
Shrieking a pitch too loud to consume
Releasing the sounds of passion
Expelled beneath a full moon

Curiosity Killed the Cat

He is not hers and he knows it
The band he wears . . . shows it
Embarking on unfamiliar territory
Bewitched by her charm and glory
Longing for a sip from her well
Her scent of seduction casting a spell
She's captured his body and soul
Parting lips for a sip of her tea
Nibbling on his ear, she mumbles
"Come with me"
Slowly crawling into her sheets
She sheds away his threads
Piercing his neck with her teeth
Removing his faculty of speech
He moans from the soothing torment
Covering every inch of him with her scent
She slithers his penis inside
Sporadically pulsating her muscles
His lids envelope his eyes
Growing tired of his silence
She unleashes her wild side
Accelerating her hip work
Provoking him to scream

Their cavities clash together
Bearing a sound so serene
Their earthquake causes a quiver
When his oil slicks her crevice
Forming a wicked smile of pleasure
As she disembarks the ride
Cuddling until the sun breaks
He's ruined his pledge to his bride
His allegiance is in jeopardy
Failing to be "The Mrs." better half
Knowing there's no turning back
Someone should've told him . . .
Curiosity killed the Cat

Oblivious

My eyes are wide opened
My mouth closed shut
A vision of exemplary beauty
Walks by with a strut
His shoes exclaim comfort
His dress code says elegant
He utters a few words
His speech is so eloquent
His teeth like white pearls
His charm I'm embracing
My heart palpitates
My blood is speed racing
Reality sinks in
He was just passing by
Never said a word to me
I didn't even catch his eye

Merry Fucking Christmas

Christmas time is here
I've gotten him an ass full of joy
And a pussy full of cheer
He likes my toss salad
Says the pussy taste like turkey
I suck 'til he releases his gravy
Celebrating the season is savory

The Back

He said "Simmer down
Today . . . I'll work your back"
To tranquilize me
He lays me on my belly
Giving me a deep tissue massage
From my neck to the small of my back
To my ass and on to my thighs
Never forgetting the pressure points of my feet
What comes next, I dare to repeat
Suddenly, he begins kissing and licking my derriere
Then, he whispers in my ear, "Unwind"
Continuing with, "Stay still"
Then, placing his index finger in my behind
Inserting it in my anus
I was told you should pain this
Yet, I'm in ecstasy by this new experience
The course he took was gentle and polite
As he engages me out of my sight
I'm stunned and bewildered
Uncertain of my next move
Screams of passion liberate my body
Nectar escapes me from below
I cum once or twice
With a puzzled face only asking one question
Who knew . . . anal fingering could feel so nice?

Skills on Wheels

Rolling down the Interstate
With our bodies feeling tight
Automobile all by itself
Pull over to the Rest Stop
Sliding out of the driver's seat
Positioning myself on his thighs
Now the car's body rocking
Ass grinding against my guy
Every stroke feeling deeper
'Til we notice a pair of eyes
Taking in the show
With a look of surprise
One would suggest we go
Yet, him watching my bounce
Has my pussy boiling hot
I don't care that I'm seen
My man's just reached the G-Spot
Though he's tensing like a bitch
Pulling out his dick
Worried about the police
Now back in my seat
Driving off in a mad dash
Back on the Interstate
All we can do is laugh

Cami

I am the reason for the rise of the sun
The midnight glow of the moon
Rays of light always shine upon me
I am Cami, you see

I'm the reason your man rises below
The reason she's envious
And her green's starting to show
I am Cami, you see

Young boys anxiously await their chance
Young girls adore my strut and stance
I'm who he wants and she wants to be
I am Cami, you see

Always my father's angel
My mother can't stand me
Together they chiseled a work of art
I am Cami, you see

This is just an introduction
A snippet of my pedigree
My wild tales are worth hearing
I am Cami, you see

About the Author

Xia Devore is a "Generation X" freelance writer and poet, hailing from Louisiana. A true Southern Girl, whose poetry reflects the Cajun spices she endures by spawning romance and erotica in her lyrics. A professional by day and poet by night, she's educated in the science of human and social behavior. Xia's love for the desires of the mind, body, and soul along with her cunning method of expression, forced her hand to write. She's a proud mother of one and a respected gardener of summer vegetables and herbs. She's a bona fide believer in love, passion, and sexual freedom.